In Dubai, less than [...] Emirati – the oth[...] country 'home'. H[...] particular, struggle [...] and friends behind a[...] a helpful book. Reb[...] [...]odewaard has written for those of us living in foreign lands and also those who move in-country to a new town or are students living away from home. Her advice is practical, centered on Christ and biblically sound with examples from her own experience and great saints of old beautifully weaved throughout the book. This book will encourage women in all stages of life to, not only survive a move, but to thrive in a new home.

Keri Folmar,
Pastor's wife from Dubai, formerly chief counsel of the
House Judiciary Subcommittee on the Constitution
Dubai, United Arab Emirates

Students, missionaries, pastors and pastor's wives, trans-ferred employees, and mothers a long way from grand-mothers—many of us experience homesickness. Rebecca VanDoodewaard has written a book full of sympathy and wisdom for them all. She has both felt homesick and helped others feeling it in university and seminary settings. Her book guides us through the pitfalls and opportunities of leaving behind the precious and familiar. Above all, it gently reminds Christians that on earth they are always pilgrims on their way to a heavenly home, the only true paradise.

Joel R. Beeke,
President, Puritan Reformed Theological Seminary,
Grand Rapids, Michigan

Much of this book reads as a manual for life situations, giving very good advice on a number of areas, including the need for spiritual preparation prior to moving; farewelling people and the need to prioritise; meditating on God's word; the importance of the church family; taking action rather than moping; and avoiding bitterness and laziness. Especially for those who move often, there is the reminder that adapting to new locations is a spiritual as well as a geographical exercise.

Mairi Harman,
Mother of 5, grandmother of 13 who enjoys assisting her
husband Allan in his ministry
Ocean Grove, Australia

Uprooted

A Guide for Homesick Christians

REBECCA VANDOODEWAARD

CHRISTIAN
FOCUS

Copyright © Rebecca VanDoodewaard 2012

paperback ISBN 978-1-84550-964-4
epub ISBN 978-1-78191-126-6
Mobi ISBN 978-1-78191-127-3

Published in 2012
by
Christian Focus Publications, Ltd.
Geanies House, Fearn, Ross-shire,
IV20 1TW, Scotland, United Kingdom.
www.christianfocus.com

Cover design by Daniel van Straaten

Printed by Nørhaven, Denmark

CONTENTS

To my parents, who taught me how to move,
and to Bill, who takes me with him.

Thanks for all the Kleenex, hugs, and prayer.

1

How I got homesick

I've moved a lot. Not as much as some military wives, but still, a lot. Once every two to three years, on average. When I was six, my family moved a thousand miles inland from the Canadian east coast. It was the first move I really remember, and it was tough; my mother spent many evenings mopping up the tears. But later moves came and went with minimal trauma. I started thinking that homesickness was for kids – or the faint of heart.

Then, when I was married with a baby, we moved from Scotland to the midwest United States: from mountains, castles, and the sea, to flatness, Wal-Mart, and a creek full of pop bottles. That was hard. I cried for nights on end, after my husband had fallen asleep. I wanted out – preferably back to Scotland. But even Canada would do! I hated where I was, and loved where I had been. And nobody except my husband even understood what I had left. Half the time I did not know how to answer the question, 'Where are you from?' because I had lived in so many places. A terrible feeling of rootlessness set in.

But there I was, so I had to learn to cope. There had to be a good book on homesickness, I thought, and my husband really needs me to read one. Amazon, Google, Christian Book Distributors, nobody seemed to have anything. So began the hard work of dealing with homesickness from the roots up: praying, studying Scripture, working, and reading biographies of other Christians who had moved and struggled with missing 'home.'

Years later, homesickness is still something that rears its ugly head, especially after a move. But the praying and studying have done what God designed them to do; God uses them to give me the grace to deal with it. I do not have implacable fortitude, a disconnect from the people around me that prevents emotional attachments, or some super-spiritual power to disregard the stuff of this earth – homes, places, things. But the Lord has given me better things: fierce closeness to my husband and children, friendships with people in many places, a better knowledge of the 'cloud of witnesses' that has gone before, and, most of all, a closer walk with Him.

Two hundred years ago, most people were born in the same area where they lived, married and died. It was unusual to move far away. Today, in a global village, people relocate for many reasons, most people several times during their lives. In my travels I have met people who have moved to the other side of the world, and sometimes back again. Whether that was from Ghana to England, Canada to South Africa, Australia to Washington, D.C., or the Netherlands to Suriname, everyone struggles with missing where they came from. Some move for career reasons, some because of a call to the ministry, some are studying, others are fleeing persecution, poverty, or war. But regardless of the cause, a move spawns homesickness to some extent. It is an issue that millions of people deal with all over the world.

Why do we get homesick? How can a new, unfamiliar place and people create such turmoil in us? Isn't it strange that exploring a new place and meeting new people can be so disjointing? Why do we long for a place to put down roots and for lasting relationships with the people around us? Because that is the way God made us. We are fearfully and wonderfully made, but we are also dust, and upheaval and change shake us. Moving can expose sin; homesickness shows just how weak we are. But it also shows something else.

When God made Adam, He set him in a divinely created home, with a perfect companion. When Adam fell, part of the punishment was leaving that home – God drove Adam and Eve out of paradise. Now, no earthly home is like that Garden, but a longing for a permanent, stable, beautiful home is within all of us. We will never find it on this earth.

King David said that 'we are strangers before [the Lord] and sojourners, as all our fathers were' (1 Chron. 29:15). Our days on the earth are like a shadow, and there is no abiding. And that is where homesickness can actually help us. As John 'Rabbi' Duncan, the great nineteenth-century Free Church minister and professor, said, 'We are on a solemn journey at all times; and the direction we are taking is of far greater consequence than the point we have reached.' Homesickness reminds us that God created us eternal beings, with eternity in our hearts. Author and Eternal Perspectives ministry director Randy Alcorn said that 'We were made for a person and a place. Jesus is the Person. Heaven is the Place. We'll never be satisfied with any person less than Jesus, and no place less than heaven. We won't be fully content until we're home with our Beloved.'

It is all right to feel homesick in an earthly sense – to miss family and friends, even places and houses – but if that is where it ends, it will simply be a bitter and empty thing. But when, through prayer and reliance on God, we use our homesickness to remind us of spiritual realities, it can actually be a blessing. The very things that are so hard about moving and living far away are the same things that can, by grace, be catalysts for spiritual growth and development. God is good to allow us feelings that bring us to the end of ourselves. When we put our homesickness to good use, it can become a tool that shapes us more and more into the image of Christ.

My homesickness is not over. It probably never will be. But looking back at what I have gained from the work and the tears, and knowing that there is probably more in store, it is all well worth it. This book does not cover every aspect of homesickness; everyone's situation and experience are unique, and this one flows out of my family's experience. I have left out some very difficult aspects of being homesick, including the death of a spouse, a broken relationship, or the move that comes in old age when you need to leave the home in which you raised your family. What this book does do is offer some strategies and principles to help you deal with your own homesickness by noting unhelpful responses, temptations in homesickness, helpful responses, and a few particular situations that can aggravate homesickness. This book is simply an attempt to help you learn some of the things that I have over the many moves, and, hopefully, to bless your soul in similar ways.

2

What is homesickness?

Webster's dictionary defines homesickness as, 'Longing for home and family while absent from them.' That's okay as far as it goes. But it does not capture the full force of the term, as you will know if you have ever felt physically ill because of the 'longing'. Homesickness can actually become a true physical 'sickness' – people can end up at the doctor because the stress of being away from those you love can place significant strain on your body. The *Journal of the American Academy of Pediatrics* recognizes that homesickness can create 'functional impairment caused by an actual or anticipated separation from home.' Amy Carmichael, the famous nineteenth-century missionary to India, referred to homesickness in shorthand – 'H.S.' was a kind of monster that attacked her at random times.

A friend from Brazil pointed out to me that people should always begin the process of dealing with homesickness by asking themselves why they are homesick. Sometimes there are reasonable causes, but other times, homesickness is a mask for sin. For instance, I know of one woman who felt terribly homesick until someone confronted her about it; it soon became clear that the only thing she missed was her mother mediating when she fought with her husband. A new place might expose an old sin. Once sin is cleared away, sometimes 'homesickness' disappears, too.

But most homesickness is caused by the pain of moving away from people and places we love, and is very real. Leaving home can be a difficult business. Susanna Spurgeon wrote, on moving away from a home she had lived in for more than two decades, 'It is hard to leave all these sympathetic surroundings and dwell in the house of a stranger, but we have seen the cloudy pillar move, and heard our Leader's voice bidding us 'go forward,' so in trustful obedience we strike our tent and prepare to depart to the 'place of which He has told us.'

And homesickness might not just be missing 'home and family'. Those are the common causes of wanting to be 'back', but a host of other things can trigger a similar response. Customs, food, language, climate, church, topography, architecture, clothing, and so on, can all aggravate the feeling of being a stranger. Everything where you are now is different, and you just want the familiar again, even for a little while.

Wanting to fit in where you do not can also create homesickness. Having a different accent, skin colour, or body shape can mark you as the outsider; people can see that you are from somewhere else, and they treat you as 'the foreigner'. Even if you are enjoying the place and the culture, having people single you out as the outsider makes it hard to feel at home.

Homesickness can be caused by the real or perceived aspects of life in the place you are now. Perhaps you came from a beautiful place, and this one seems ugly. Maybe it has a climate that you are not used to. Maybe the days seem to drag by, or maybe everyone around you seems to be rushing and you cannot keep up with the pace. When students move into the city where we live, we marvel at how differently they respond to the same place. People from large Asian cities find it rural and a little out of date – almost cute. But students from the African countryside see a high-tech, cold and sterile metropolis. Where you came from has a huge impact on how you view where you are now. It might not be that where you came from was that great, but simply that where you are now is so strange or difficult. You do not want to be 'back' because you loved it; you just hate where you are, and going back seems like a reasonable way out of your situation.

Living away from home during school, short term missions, long hospital stays, or any number of other temporary situations can create homesickness. My sister always cries the first night away from home, whether she is in Amman, Jordan, where she went to work in the slums for a summer, or at a weekend conference with her husband, a couple of hours away from their apartment. A situation that presents totally new surroundings and people is almost always daunting, and can make you long for the familiar and comfortable, even if you are only facing the new for a while.

But homesickness is the worst when you move. Then, you do not miss home 'when' you are absent, as the dictionary says; you miss it all the time, because you will be absent for good. You do not live there anymore, and the living there is what you ache for; the day-to-day social interactions and routines that are familiar, comfortable, comforting, pleasant, maybe even stimulating or energizing. The loss of knowing and being known hurts.

For some people, though, it does not stop there. There is such a thing as complicated homesickness:

missing multiple groups of people, places or cultures because you have lived in multiple places. Wanting a certain church building in another setting filled with people speaking another language is possible. And it can get pretty complicated. It is even possible to want to be in two places at the same time, even when there is nothing special going on!

There is also the time after every move when you do not feel entirely at home in any place. I have a friend who moved from England to Canada. After a few years in her new home, she told me that though she often felt like a foreigner in Canada, she no longer felt at home in the U.K. 'Wherever I go, people think of me as the person from somewhere else; the new place is still not home, and when I go back to England, so many little things have changed – in the people and the area – that I feel like a stranger. It's a kind of no-man's land.'

Certain events or times can aggravate home-sickness as well. Being sick with no family or friends to help can be isolating. Being ill is hard, but being ill without sympathy, meals, and maybe a good babysitter is lonely as well. The occurrence of birthdays, anniversaries, or other events back home can emphasize distance. Having a sister get married and not be able to be involved with the preparations, showers, and shopping, can trigger a severe bout of homesickness for women. A parent

19

who is dying far away, a brother who is suffering, a close friend who is having a baby: all can make you feel distanced – unable to rejoice with those who rejoice and mourn with those who mourn. This can make you feel helpless and disconnected.

Homesickness can come as grief, boredom, fear, frustration, depression, or any number of expressions, depending on your personality. But all of these forms of homesickness, no matter what the particular cause, can sidetrack you. They distract you from your calling, suck away joy, and frustrate you. That is because homesickness, while in itself not a sin, can quickly turn into discontentment. When your desires and wants and longings stop you from seeing the opportunities, lessons, work, and blessings where the Lord has put you, homesickness becomes spiritually crippling. That is why we need to see it as a danger that should be dealt with as quickly and biblically as possible.

3

What to do before
you leave

Fighting homesickness begins before a move. If you know you are going to be moving, start preparing yourself while you pack. Just like planning when and where you are going to move is necessary to the physical success of a move, so preparation for the other challenges, including homesickness, will make the move easier.

Spiritual preparation is the most important aspect of fighting homesickness. If your soul is not still and quiet before the Lord (Ps. 131:2), this move will be turbulent, whether or not you have professional movers doing the work. Even if you know this move is a good thing and want to do it, it is going to cut off a lot of your roots – it will deracinate you. Be grounded in your identity as one of God's children who is constantly in the Father's care. You need to be secure in and consciously aware of the Lord's providence; if this is His will for you, there is no better place you can be. Remind yourself of this truth, and rest in it.

Another important pre-move practice is prayer. Pray that the Lord would prepare you to make this move to His glory. Ask Him for the strength to go through all the work ahead. Pray that He would provide a congregation for you in your new location – people who will love you, minister to you, and whom you can also serve once you are settled.

It is also helpful to recognize upfront that moving takes a lot of mental and emotional effort, over and above the physical work. This is true even before you actually move; the emotional drain begins when you realize you will be moving. One move that we went through was particularly stressful; there were family weddings immediately before and after which involved international trips with small children, saying goodbye to a congregation we loved, driving hundreds of miles, arriving at a filthy house, enormous amounts of company immediately, plus the normal work that comes with a move. I ploughed ahead through it all, furiously checking items off my lists, going through customs with toddlers, whipping together meals for guests – and I ended up at the doctor with burnout.

Since then, we have been more careful to build 'down times' into a move. Even if your to-do list seems overwhelming, take breaks from packing; bring your kids to the park, go to your favorite restaurant, and go to bed on time. If you have a long drive to your new home, plan a few stops along the way. After you arrive, do not feel like you have to unpack everything in two days – or even two weeks! As much as possible, make the work of moving pleasant, not stressful. Keep at the work and get it out of the way, but do not make yourself or your family miserable doing it. Know that moving often hits you hard mentally and emotionally, and build in 'cushions' to help you absorb the impact.

As you look ahead to a move, prepare yourself emotionally for new friendships with people. You may not feel as though you need or even want to develop relationships with people whom you do not know right now, but it will be a part of life once you land. Be ready to befriend people and have them befriend you.

Saying goodbye is the hardest part before a move. Different people say goodbye in different ways, and the strong emotions that come with leaving loved people and places will express themselves according to personality. Some people weep openly. Some do not react strongly; they try and 'keep it together' for the sake of those around them. But no matter how you express your emotion, saying goodbye is a difficult thing.

23

There are roughly three different kinds of people whom you will say goodbye to: acquaintances, 'general' friends, and close friends and family. Acquaintances are the easiest to say goodbye to. A simple, 'It's been good to know you,' or 'I hope things go well for your family,' can be sincere and sufficient. For 'general' friends – people in your church or neighborhood who spend some time with you but are not extremely close – one good way of saying goodbye is a pot-luck, group picnic, or some other venue where you can have mini-visits with each person or family, saying goodbye to each as they leave when the event is over.

Saying goodbye to close friends and family demands the most emotional energy, time, and thought. Before each move we have deliberately spent more time with family or close friends, not simply talking about the move, but about life, the Lord, and the other things which connect us. Sometimes we have spent our last meal in a town with family or friends with the moving truck parked and loaded in the driveway.

I like to give a small, meaningful gift to close family or friends during our last visit. A note saying how much they mean to you is a great way to not only say goodbye but also strengthen your friendship even as you leave. A 'thank-you book' – a notebook in which you have written down individual thank-you notes for everything a person has done for you – is a thoughtful present. Perhaps something little they admired in your home can be wrapped and brought to their home instead of packed. Try to communicate your love and appreciation for these people to them before you head out, building the relationship before a separation.

If you have children, clearly explain what is going on, and that it is important for them to say goodbye, especially to family, even if they would rather let you do the emotional work for them. It is just as important for them to learn to do this as it is for them to show their love to the people who are staying behind.

Saying goodbye to older family or friends is the hardest: they might not be living the next time you come to visit. This is where the promises of heaven are the most precious. Remember that, if the people you are leaving are believers, you will spend eternity together; this is a temporary, earthly parting. It is sad, yes, and sometimes heartbreaking, but it is not the ultimate. If the elderly or terminally ill people whom you are leaving are not believers, use this opportunity to press home the claims of Christ to them one last time, face to face. Tell them you will be praying for them. There is nothing else you can do but rest in the Lord's dealings with them and with you; His ways are higher than our ways, and will ultimately bring Him glory (Isa. 55:9).

In the emotion of saying goodbye, do not promise impossible things. Establishing unrealistic goals for maintaining old relationships will set you up for homesickness when you cannot meet your expectations. If you are moving to Outer Mongolia on a small salary, do not say that you will fly back twice a year. Tell them you will visit when you can. If you will be home schooling six children, do not promise to call a friend every day. Say that you will stay in touch. Communicate that you will do what you can to maintain the relationship, making sure that what you have committed to will be possible and helpful to both sides.

Sometimes having the process of saying goodbye behind you is actually a relief in itself. All the tension, the dread, and perhaps some awkwardness are over once you are on the road. In most of our moves, we have found that the excitement of the move begins when the last person has been kissed, hugged, and prayed with, and we are travelling together as a family. Sometimes we are crying as we leave, but the promise of a new start and the Lord's leading have been encouragements even as we grieve separations.

Keep an open mind as you head into this new experience; not everything will be the way you expect or hope that it will. But when you remember that the Lord has ordained everything – that He already knows exactly how everything will work out – you will be able to face this challenge with cheerfulness and courage.

4

What makes homesickness worse?

At a large university, I used to work with international exchange students who arrived in new batches every fall, jet-lagged, nervous, and clutching their passports. They came from all over the world: China, Bahamas, Malta, Ethiopia, Ireland, South Korea, and elsewhere. The university staff team always told them that the hardest point in dealing with homesickness would usually be around three months: the excitement of being somewhere new would have worn off, and nothing here would be comfortably familiar yet. But long before the three-month mark, the team could pick out those who would not last the year. These students fed their homesickness, sometimes bringing it to a climax with a mid-semester flight home. They all did the same, very unhelpful things that we had warned them against.

Although homesickness may be a natural response to a change in location or circumstances, it can be made better or worse based on how we respond to it. Just as eating hamburgers when you have the flu would delay recovery, so there are activities that can make homesickness last longer, and even increase it. The following guidelines are ones that we gave to international students year after year; I have added some ideas specifically for believers.

Do not sit on the couch looking at pictures of home. For one thing, a lack of exercise can aggravate emotional downs. But more importantly, the pictures are not going to help you. When you are cheerful, they might remind you of pleasant memories or encourage you to pray for people, but if you are already depressed, meditating on what you have lost will sink you further into despair. The pictures do not have to be physical; you can mull pictures in your mind as well, constantly going back in your imagination. The results will be the same. Meditate on the Word instead, and pray for the people whom you miss.

Do not spend hours on the phone with people back home. Calling people you have left once in a while to find out how they are and what is going on is good, but developing an emotional addiction (and it *can* be an addiction) to 'fellowship' with people hundreds or thousands of miles away will stunt relationships and productivity in your new location. Use calls back home to stay current with things there and to update people there on your life. Do not use your phone like a drug to anesthetize your homesickness.

Do not allow frustrations with the new place and people to grow. Yes, it might rain everyday: that is why your lawn is so green. Yes, everybody might wear camo or sweatpants: they have no need for anything else. Seeing the bad in everything is not only unhelpful; it is wrong. God made the people in His image, and He created the place for His glory. Yes, both have sin, and so do you. Remember that common grace extends throughout the world, and look for it where you are. Also remember that, because God made these people and is working His grace in the Church here, there is something you can learn from these folk. If the people around you are believers, they will know things about the Lord and the Christian life – let alone everyday life – that you do not. Do not cut yourself off from this source of spiritual nourishment and common sense just because it comes in a different package than you are used to.

Do not idealize the place where you used to be. It might have been easier for you there, but it was not a resort with room service, free food and perfect weather. You got hungry and cold there, got speeding tickets, spilled things on your shirt, made trips to the emergency room, attended funerals, and experienced all kinds of other difficulties. Just because there are things that you have a hard time with in the new place does not mean that you can forget that the main reason the old place seems great is probably because you were used to it.

Do not spoil social attachments by constantly telling people that you are homesick, that you miss everyone at 'home', and that you want to go back. This will not help you. It is good to honestly tell friends who ask that you are having a tough time adjusting, but it is not all right to whine everywhere about your homesickness. Whether it is a way to get attention or simply an overflow of strong emotion, telling everyone how you feel is not going to help you. People truly appreciate fortitude; it will strengthen relationships in your new place. Maggie Paton, after decades of service in the New Hebrides, had a native woman come up to her and say, 'Missi, you did not think we felt like you. You never told us your troubles. You used to smile, when you spoke of your children in the far-off Land when we knew your heart was crying out for them. We knew the language of your heart, Missi, though you tried to hide it from us.' Just as people recognize and appreciate bravery, so a lack of self-control is obvious and repellant.

Do not think about yourself all the time. How do I feel? Do I like it here? Do people like me? Do I want to go home? These are profoundly unhelpful things to ask, since the answers, likely sad ones, will not fix your situation. Instead of constantly prioritizing yourself and your needs, start thinking about the people around you and the work that is in front of you.

Lastly and most importantly, there is one thing that aggravates homesickness which takes drastic action to address: living in the wrong place. Living in 'the wrong place' does not mean the place has the wrong restaurants, the wrong weather, the wrong house. It means that there is nowhere to worship. If there is no gospel preaching, fellowshipping, accountability-providing, evangelistic congregation where you can worship and serve, then you should not be where you are at all, homesick or not. While there may be temporary, special circumstances, such as military placements, that put a solid church out of reach, studies, ordinary careers, and comfortable homes must come behind gospel preaching and fellowship in our list of priorities. We may have to spend a lot of time in the car in order to be in a good place Sunday mornings, but our spiritual health is at stake. The process of finding a place to worship can be difficult and emphasize homesickness, as you long for the congregation you have left. A new church, even when it is solidly biblical, will likely come in a different package than you are used to, and it often takes time to see past cultural differences to spiritual and theological oneness. But even when the church takes some time to adjust to, there needs to be one, unless you have been sent as a missionary. Where there is no solid church, you will spiritually wither, making survival in the new place a façade at best. Mary Winslow once counseled a friend who was looking for a home in a new place,

> While you are debating in your mind where you shall fix your abode, you will insensibly be a loser and your heart will grow cold unless your eye and heart are ever toward Jesus. In choosing your place of residence, consult the Lord, and pitch your tent nowhere where you cannot hear the gospel in all its purity and sweet simplicity. Remember Lot's great mistake! He pitched his tent towards Sodom because it pleased his carnal nature; and God, for this, stripped him of all, and he barely escaped with his life. The Lord has given us instructions how to walk before a gainsaying world; and if we depart, he will chasten us with the rod, nevertheless, he will never leave us or forsake us. Do not, I charge you dear sister, make your dwelling where the gospel is not faithfully preached, and where the ordinances of Christ

are dishonoured...Let not house nor pleasant
prospect be your first aim. Seek *first* the kingdom
of God and His righteousness, and God will bless
you and make you a blessing.

In other words, if you are not where God wants
you, you cannot expect Him to bless you. If you are
in a spiritually dry place, with few opportunities to
serve, then you can fight homesickness tooth and
nail, checking off all the recommendations above,
and you will only wither. In short, unless you have
been sent to the mission field, you will have to
move.

While not doing these things does not guarantee
the absence of homesickness, it may help alleviate
it, or at least keep you from making it worse. The
international students at my university who worked
on avoiding these activities tended to flourish; one
Japanese student had a thriving social life, scored
perfectly on his business final, and took a rich
cultural experience back with him to Japan. The
students who continued unhelpful behavior often
suffered bad grades, depression, sickness, and even
gave up on their studies and flew home, damaging
much more than their transcripts.

If you are in a place where you can be fed and
serve the church, then these ideas should help you.
Prayerfully following them should make you less

homesick and so even more fruitful where the Lord has put you. Remember that the hardest part of homesickness is near the beginning, what missionary George Leslie Mackay called, 'those first, friendless days'. Homesickness may never end, but by grace, it will get easier as you become better at dealing with it biblically.

5

Temptations in homesickness

The list of actions to avoid provided in the previous chapter might make it sound like fighting homesickness is easy. It is not. There are many temptations that can creep in and 'get' you when you least expect it. Even Baptist missionary Ann Judson, with her driving sense of call and purpose, wrote during her voyage away from America, 'My native land, my home, my friends, and all my former enjoyments, rushed into my mind; my tears flowed profusely, and I could not be comforted'.

The presence of temptation is not sin; it is evidence of Satan's work. It becomes sin when we succumb to what the temptation offers. Satan knows that a discouraged person is the perfect target for temptation, and also that resisting repeated temptations is discouraging. So be on your guard against temptation, remembering that our Lord 'who in every respect has been tempted as we are', was 'yet without sin' (Heb. 4:15). Confess your temptations to the Lord and cry out for His grace to overcome the sin which so easily entangles (Heb. 12:1). Remember that our Lord responded to the temptations He faced with the sword of the Word; study of the Scriptures and prayers for the Spirit's protection will enable you to fight the following temptations, even when you are homesick.

In the West, we are told all the time that life should be easy, that we deserve a break, that we need to take it easy. Life is not like that, but when you are told that is how it should be, complaining about circumstances, places, and people can become a default position. But Scripture anticipates our grumbling spirits with the call to 'Do all things without grumbling or disputing' (Phil. 2:14). *All* things – no qualifications! That includes living in a new place, no matter how many, great, and frequent the inconveniences are. Do not complain.

Some personalities will be tempted to ignore the homesickness they feel, thinking that it is a sign of weakness. But it is a sign of our humanity, not of personal weakness. George Leslie Mackay, a Victorian-era, Canadian missionary to Taiwan, suffered from homesickness for his twenty-three years on the field. For more than two decades, he 'looked back from far Formosa, [and] in fancy gazed upon my Zorra home'. This emotion came from a man who cut through hundreds of miles of jungle to pull tens of thousands of rotten teeth, preached hundreds of sermons, and sailed around the world half a dozen times. The natives called him 'the black-bearded barbarian' – Mackay was no wimp. Admitting that you are homesick, instead of bottling it up in pride, can actually help you deal with the emotion.

Bitterness is perhaps a temptation that attacks women more than men. We tend by nature to be more sensitive, to get hurt easily and to remember well. When this is not tempered by thankfulness, forgiveness, and humility, it grows into bitterness – an ugly fruit that can poison a person's entire life, turning them away from the Lord, distancing them from their family, and stunting new relationships. If you are married, do not grow bitter towards your spouse for taking you to a new place. Turning in on yourself in bitterness will only create distance between you and your closest companion in a time when both of you need an understanding, cheerful spouse. Do not grow bitter towards old friends for not staying in touch. This will only isolate you further

37

and sink you deeper into discouragement. And do not grow bitter towards the Lord for leading you to where He has. Bitterness is something that we need to fight off through frequent, fervent prayer.

A fourth area of temptation is laziness. How can someone who has moved to a new place, set up a new house and navigated a new grocery store be lazy? By calling it quits after the essential work is done. You think, 'I've moved, I've done so much, dealt with a lot of emotions. I can't do anything else.' But you can. And you must. Do not put the onus on other people to pick up the slack, either in your family or the church. 'Do not grow weary in doing good,' the apostle urges the Thessalonians and us (2 Thess. 3:13). Galatians 6:9 promises that 'in due season we will reap, if we do not give up'. God will always give you the grace you need to do the necessary and good works which he has prepared in advance for us, whether that is visiting a widow, bringing someone a meal, or any other good work that your hand finds to do. Trust Him for grace and strength, and get to work. At the seminary where my husband teaches, one new student couple astounded us by helping nearly every other new student unload moving trucks and unpack boxes in the weeks following their own long-distance move. This couple, though they must have been tired, became one of the best-adjusted families in the seminary by the time classes began, reaping friendships and love from the work they had sown.

Moving to a new place can be exciting, but it can be overwhelmingly busy. Finding the library, switching your driver's license, setting up a new home, and remembering all the names of people you meet can be draining and make any homesickness worse. Hiding out in your house – the only truly familiar place – might be appealing. Being a hermit can seem like an escape from everything, and a step closer to your old home. In reality, though, it only delays the work of adjustment and cuts you off from the work and opportunities that the Lord has for you. The real way to fight the temptation of hiding at home is to recognize it, and to get out, meet the people, navigate the streets, and wade through the paper work – and then to take a break and enjoy!

Living in the past is a temptation that can be closely tied to being a hermit. The present is no fun, the past seems appealing, so you constantly think of, talk about, and maybe try to reconstruct things that you did in the place you used to live. Like being a recluse, this will distance you from the people and happenings in your new location. There are fewer things more dull than listening to someone talk endlessly about how 'after Susan said that, she went into the kitchen where my mom was, and then my brother got home from work with some fresh milk....' And so on for hours. This is a denial of the reality in which God has placed you. Focus on where you are, what you should be doing, and who you are interacting with here and now.

One last temptation in homesickness is to compare your new location and people with the ones you just left. Comparison itself is not sinful, and can even be fun, but it can also be symptomatic of envy, discontentment, or other sins. Saying things like, 'His mannerisms remind me so much of my dad!' is not wrong, but constant, unfavorable compare-and-contrast sessions will cripple you in loving the people and place where God has providentially put you. Thoughts like 'A handshake makes so much more sense than a bow' or 'This preacher should learn to gesture like my former pastor did' will lead to frustration – another enemy to joy and contentment. Ann Judson noted that 'recollection of former enjoyments, in my own native country, made my situation here appear less tolerable'. Being patient and humble in your circumstances and with the people you meet will go a long way in fostering fruitfulness and happiness in your new home.

Above all, remember that without Christ you cannot fight temptation. It always wins out against natural strength, because even when our spirit is willing, the flesh is weak (Mark 14:38). A homesick person, often physically and emotionally tired, is quite vulnerable. Praise God, who has enabled us to 'do all things through him who strengthens me' (Phil. 4:13), and taught us to pray, 'lead us not into temptation' (Matt. 6:13). He can deliver us from every temptation. And remember that no temptation faces you except that which is common to man (1 Cor. 10:13). Do not think that you are the only one who has endured these emotions, or endured them to this extent. You are not. There are people who have moved further, lost more and suffered more deeply than you have. Thank the Lord for His grace to you.

6

What makes homesickness better?

Thankfully, homesickness is not just something that runs us over and leaves us flat. It can, if we do nothing about it, but there are ways to fight it. Studying the Word, talking with other believers, and reading biographies of those who have gone before allow some clear strategies to emerge for dealing with deracination. In order of importance, here are a dozen ways to lessen homesickness.

First, pray. Pray with thanks that the Lord has brought you to this place, and acknowledge His leading and providential care for you. Pour out your anxieties and griefs to Him – He has been tempted in every way as you have, and He remembers your frame. He knows that you are dust. Cast all your cares on Him, for He cares for you (1 Pet. 5:7). Pray that you would be fruitful where you are, and ask God to bless you in your new location. Susanna Spurgeon observed that '[O]ur new home may be to us a 'Tabor' if our Lord will but dwell with us there.' Fellowshipping with and seeking the Lord in prayer is the first and most important step in fighting homesickness.

Be in the Word. Read it morning, noon and night. If you are married, read it with your spouse. If you have kids, read it with them, too. Choose a certain book of the Bible to dig into on your own – a gospel, maybe – and find a good sermon series to augment your reading. Find a Bible reading plan (chronological, concurrent Testaments, etc.) and try and stick to the program to read through the Bible in a year. You need the whole counsel of God in truckloads when your life is so disrupted.

Meditating on Christ's life on earth is a third way to fight homesickness. While here, the Westminster Shorter Catechism Answer 27 explains, our Savior lived a life of poverty and suffering. And He did not complain. He did not become bitter. He did not demand service from people, but rather threw Himself into serving others. He did not become introverted. Of all people who have ever moved, Christ went from the greater to the unspeakably lesser, with no place to lay His head (Matt. 8:20).

He was not simply torn a literal world away from His Father, but the people to whom He came also rejected Him to the point of killing Him. And still, He remained faithful to the calling which the Trinity had agreed upon for the salvation of the elect. Hudson Taylor wrote of leaving his mother on shore while he boarded the ship that took him to China:

> I shall never forget that cry of anguish wrung from a mother's heart. It went through me like a knife. I never knew so fully, until then, what 'God so loved the world' meant.

Remembering Christ's work for you, applying it to your life, and meditating on the cross, will put any move into perspective and give you renewed joy in your calling, wherever that may be. It will also draw you closer to your Savior.

Fourth, if you have family with you, serve them. Lead them in family worship, or support your husband as he leads. If you are a husband and father, work diligently to provide for your family's physical needs. Attend to your wife, who probably needs extra love and affection after following you away from family and friends. Remember that it is your calling to shepherd your family through the transitions. If you are a wife or mother, serve your husband by supporting him in his leadership. Exert yourself in controlling your emotions; be cheerful instead of bitter or sad. A move is a wonderful opportunity for a husband and wife to grow closer together. In our marriage, the Lord has used every relocation to draw us closer as a couple: hard work and cheerfulness during struggles earn mutual respect in new places where we have no other earthly help. A kiss in between carrying boxes, a 'thank you' at dinner, and a shared search for sheets at bedtime are things that make a move more pleasant and a marriage stronger. If you have kids, show them lots of love as they adjust to new settings and new people. Serve them by making your new house a clean and attractive home, a haven in a strange place. 'Home,' Maggie Paton wrote, 'has so much influence on one's work, and on life and character; it is due to our wee boys to make it a bright one.'

The fifth way to fight homesickness is to become involved and accountable in a local, Bible-believing, gospel preaching, evangelical church. The church is the body of Christ, and if you are not connected to it, you will suffer. You need the preached word and ministry of the sacraments to feed your soul. Without them, you will shrivel up, even with private Scripture reading and prayer during the week. Neglecting the local church will also likely turn you in on yourself. It is easy to feel sorry for yourself when you are homesick and do not really know anyone else. Being plugged into a local congregation where the person in front of you has cancer, the teenager across the aisle is dealing with divorcing parents, and the congregation has other struggles and joys will put your own situation in perspective and connect you to people whom you can serve. A good local church will give you fellowship, too; people who will love you, care for you, bear your burdens, encourage you, and, when you need it, rebuke you. The Psalmist declares that being a servant by the entrance to the Lord's courts is far better than dwelling (i.e., having a permanent home) in tents of wickedness (Ps. 84:10). Finding a solid, local church is an essential source of joy and growth.

If your new location comes with a new language, dig in. People who shy away from the hard and often awkward work of learning a new language rarely succeed in understanding worship, building friendships, or growing at work. It is a hard and technical aspect of fighting homesickness, but it is essential. My grandmother, coming to North America from the Netherlands in her early twenties, was embarrassed to put her tongue between her teeth to make the 'th' sound. 'Then I realized,' she says, 'that I looked far more stupid not sticking my tongue out than doing it.' She still has an accent, but has adopted the idioms, colloquialisms, technical jargon and 'th' sound. Amy Carmichael struggled for years to master new languages – 'You may put it on my tomb-stone: expired in despair.' – but pressed on, determined to minister to the natives in their own language. You are never too old to learn a language; do not cut yourself off from fellowship and other blessings because of the initial work of mastering new vocabulary. If you feel at home with the language, you will feel more at home in general, and it will open many doors for service.

Whatever your vocation is, work hard at it to the glory of God. Give yourself to your job, whether that is at an office, on a field, in a classroom, or with kids in the kitchen. Paul instructs believers to 'work heartily, as for the Lord' (Col. 3:23). Hard work in your calling is a big way to bear fruit where you are, and will take your mind off of yourself and your homesickness. Maggie Paton, ministering to the natives in the New Hebrides, wrote in a letter, 'I have never known what it was to have a long day, or five minutes, to indulge in melancholy…I never knew, till coming here, what a healthy thing it is for both mind and body to have plenty to do.' Charles Spurgeon gave this advice: 'Let every believer accept this as the inference of experience: that for most human maladies the best relief and antidote will be found in self-sacrificing work for the Lord Jesus.' Homesickness is one of those maladies cured by this sort of work.

Eighth, become accountable to someone in your new location. This is part of being in a good church, but even in a good church you might have to pursue a partnership with someone in particular. Find someone wiser (and probably older) than you to ask you about your faithfulness in the Word and prayer, to your family, in your work. Seek it out – do not wait for it to come to you. Healthy accountability will help you develop a close relationship with another believer and strengthen your walk with the Lord.

Practice hospitality. Often, after a move to a new place, we feel as though other people should reach out to us. But obeying Scripture's command to practice hospitality (Rom. 12:13) by having people into your home for a meal can really kill homesickness. It focuses your attention and energy on others, allows you to serve, accelerates getting to know people, and even spurs you on in making your house a home as you organize, clean, and cook for your guests.

The tenth way to fight homesickness is to get out and do something local. Everywhere – even north-central Indiana – has something to do. Discovering the unique assets of a place can help you like it. Knowing where to go apple-picking, hiking, or antique shopping, will help you enjoy being where you are, even if it seems like a small thing. As well as the joy of exploration, coming home from a short trip will make your new house seem like a home: it will be the familiar place that you return to.

Use technology to stay in touch with your family and friends in the place you have left. In this day and age, having web access is standard unless you live in a remote, missionary setting. Use it! Once you have internet service, most e-mail accounts and almost all social media are free, so take advantage of them. Get e-mail, Facebook, Twitter accounts – whatever most of your family and friends have – so you can stay in contact with them. Open a skype or video MSN account so you can see people back home while you talk to them. You can even set up a private YouTube page so people on both sides can post videos for each other to watch. A good long-distance phone plan can be a blessing, especially when communicating with older parents, grandparents, or friends who do not use newer technology.

Lastly, learn a new skill, tackle an author's works, or develop a new hobby. God has given us so much to enjoy, and discovering His gifts can be not only a welcome distraction, but also a way to connect to your new location. My husband and I have enjoyed linking different places with different blessings in the forms of books and hobbies: Scotland is where I learned new cooking skills, Indiana is where he learned to preach, Virginia is where we learned a lot of American history and read Spurgeon. Do not simply ignore or fight the hard things the Lord gives you – take and be thankful for the good things.

God always gives us the grace to do what He calls us to, and that includes living in a new place. It is not less spiritual to use the available tools to fight homesickness than to struggle on without help or purposeful action. The Lord blesses us smoldering wicks and bruised reeds with what we need to keep going (Isa. 42:3). We need to avail ourselves of all the means, 'spiritual' and seemingly 'less spiritual', to live for His glory where He puts us. All of these ideas are simply the use of the means and opportunities that God provides; fight homesickness by faithfully doing what He has called you to where He has placed you.

7

Homesick with kids

Children can aggravate homesickness. Your own homesickness can be multiplied by seeing your kids suffering the same things. You might be going through your day fine, then find your daughter in a puddle of tears on her bed, and suddenly you are a puddle beside her.

Children will express and process homesickness differently at different ages. Toddlers can become clingy, weepy, and not sleep well for the first few weeks. School-aged kids, even if they initially saw the move as an adventure, will cry for friends and a familiar house. Teenagers may seem sullen and angry. As though you did not have enough to deal with, it seems like you now need a nouthetic counselor with a degree in child psychology on call. Moving is rough on parents and children alike.

Having no family around can be especially tough. Grandparents take interest in all the little (or not-so-little) developments, outfits, and achievements of children in a way that other people generally cannot. Ann Judson summed up her sorrow of having no family to see her infant son in a letter to her mother: 'I know, my dear mother, you long very much to see my little boy. I wish you were here to see him.' Every mother living with little ones far from family has probably felt that wishing. Living far away from people who love your kids as much as you do is hard not only because there is no one to talk to at length about childhood's many joys and sorrows, but also because you do not have the examples of godly grandparents and other family for your kids to look up to.

Sometimes you may feel guilty for taking your kids away from family and friends. Just knowing that grandparents are suffering too can depress you for separating your kids from people who love them so much. Prayer, open discussions with your parents (and kids, if they are old enough), and a trust in the Lord's leading can ameliorate this. When our oldest daughter was five months old, the only grandchild on my side of the family, we moved from Canada to Scotland. It was a great relief to know that we were doing what was best for our family. Thankfully, my parents also knew this and supported us in it, even though it was a very difficult thing for them. Over the years, staying in contact via phone, e-mail and a blog with frequently posted pictures of the kids has really helped ease this difficult aspect of homesickness and separation.

In your new location, there might be a lack of positive familial pressure on your kids to carry on the faith of their fathers. Having nearby family and friends who are watching your kids and your parenting can put a healthy pressure on your kids to be careful how they walk and talk. It can also keep you from slacking off in discipline, communication and encouragement as you parent the children that God has entrusted to you. Without these supports and safeguards, you need to be very, very aware, through prayer, Bible study and conversations with your spouse and kids, of weaknesses, struggles and spiritual needs in your family.

A lack of understanding in your new setting of the way you discipline, teach and shepherd your children can turn homesickness into loneliness. You wonder, as you haul your screaming two-year-old to a church bathroom, if anyone else understands that you are doing it for your child's good, and not because you are frustrated. When you discover that other parents allow their teens to watch new releases together every Saturday, you can feel like the strict, pharisaical parent – the only one who keeps their child away from their friends on the weekend. Or maybe you are comfortable with your child doing something that it seems everyone else condemns, and thinks you are irresponsible to allow. Again, staying in the Word, in prayer, in communication with your spouse, as well as seeking advice from older believers, can really relieve this aspect of homesickness.

Help your kids fight homesickness in the same ways you do, especially encouraging them to pray and read the Word. Tell them often that you love them. Make a point of spending unhurried time with them each day, even if it means not reaching your unpacking goal until later. Sometimes late evenings are the most productive in dealing with a homesick teenager who is silent by day. Seize the times when your kids open up to minister to them, dropping everything else to utilize this parenting opportunity. Talk about what they miss; listen to their griefs and frustrations with the new place.

Teach your kids to delight in the discovery of a new location. Do something fun with them: go to the zoo or a cultural event, try new foods, visit a tourist site, or explore a rural area nearby. Let them call an old friend regularly to maintain existing friendships. Give them lots of hugs and kisses – even boys who pretend they do not like it. Kids, even big ones, need lots of love in a new place, and you and your spouse need to be available to provide it.

Create accountability for your kids, and for yourself as a parent. Find an older (older in the faith, at least) couple who sees your family regularly and is willing to offer encouragement, challenge and rebuke as needed. You need it yourself, and your kids sometimes need counsel and challenge from a godly person outside the family. Pray that the Lord would provide a couple who will love your kids and whom your kids feel comfortable around. I do not mean a sweet, old lady who pats your son's head and remarks at his advancing height every fellowship meal. I mean a couple who will let your kids know that they love them for the Lord's sake – someone whom your kids will look up to.

Everywhere we have lived, the Lord has provided what we call 'surrogate grandparents'. They have been godly couples with wonderful marriages and older children (who often become surrogate 'aunts' and 'uncles'). These couples have cared for the souls of our children so much that they are eager to invest in the kids' lives by regularly praying for them, reading them books, inviting them to the beach, dropping off a gift on birthdays, taking them shopping, listening to long, imaginary stories from preschoolers, looking after siblings during labor and delivery, even changing diapers, and asking some tough questions! People like this will be an invaluable resource for you and for your children, because they not only encourage and bless you, but will also show the love of Christ to your kids in tangible ways. It is solid relationships like these that will, by grace, help your kids face the challenges of the teen years and provide wisdom for their adult years. Pray for surrogate grandparents.

Help your kids develop healthy relationships with peers from Christian families. In some congregations, finding good friends for your children is far more difficult than finding surrogate grandparents! Pray fervently and act decisively to help your children form their closest friendships with other covenant kids. Talk with them about the kids they meet. We have had many conversations about new acquaintances: 'What did you think about that girl? Was she kind to other kids? Why do you think she wants to be your friend? Did that boy speak respectfully to his mother? What book was he reading? Why did you like hanging out with him?'

Do not be afraid to end your child's relationship with another child who is hindering his spiritual, emotional, intellectual or social development. Nineteenth-century pastor and author John Angell James warns parents, 'At the risk of offending the nearest relative, or the most endeared friend he has on earth, a Christian parent ought not to suffer his children to associate with those who are likely to do them harm.' Do not let your chance of friendship with another parent in a new place take priority over your child's well-being. Cut off any relationship that is harming your child without fear of the repercussions it will have on you. Be active in helping them pursue friendships with godly kids: go out of your way to make time to have them over, encourage conversations at church, and, most of all, pray that the Lord would give your children friends who would sharpen them in the faith as iron sharpens iron.

When you see your kids suffering from home-sickness, remember that the Lord loves them even more than you do, and that He loves them perfectly. They are really His children, simply on loan to you. Christ, who said, 'Let the little children come to me' (Matt. 19:14), will only send your kids what is best for them, which includes homesickness. If you are tempted to distrust or question the Lord when you are weary in parenting sad kids in a new place, remember that He gently leads those who are with young (Isa. 40:11). This is a tender comfort for us as we serve the Great Shepherd by caring faithfully for our children everywhere God places us.

Moving to a new culture with kids can cause you a different kind of pain, as you see your children growing up as members of a society that still feels foreign to you, but is home to them. When we were living in the U.K., another transplanted mother told me that it hurt her to think that her kids did not know what it was to be American, despite having U.S. citizenship and accents. A Philippine mother shared her frustrations that her children were losing their first language, and did not like her cooking anymore, preferring Italian-American fare. It does not have to be that big of a move to make you realize that your children are becoming a different kind of person than you are. My kids speak the same language that I do, but they are more and more integrated into American culture: they recognize the President, but not my Prime Minister; they eat corn dogs, but not poutine; they have been up the Washington Monument several times, but never the Peace Tower.

My natural tendency is to fight this, and keep them in a cultural bubble. But this is not realistic or helpful to them. Instead, I need to create a distinctly Christian culture in our home, so that no matter what foods they enjoy, or what accent they have, citizenship of the heavenly kingdom is primary. They need to know that while I might be saddened by the distance that different cultures create, their love for the things of Christ trumps all cultural and linguistic barriers. The kingdom of heaven is made up of every tribe, tongue and nation on earth; now is a good time to learn this ourselves and to teach this truth to our children.

Giving birth to children far away from friends and family can be just as difficult as shepherding homesick children. Having a baby can cause a lot of homesickness in parents, especially mothers. Your new baby does not miss anything, but you weep that your parents cannot see this new grandchild, and that this infant will not know who they are for years. There is no sister to come to the hospital and sympathize with your labor and delivery story, no friend to drop off a pair of bitty shoes, no mother-in-law to tell you that the baby's cowlick looks just like your husband's when he was born. A strange hospital system and different medical care can make you wish you were back where you used to be, where the doctor knew what she was doing, or there was food available in the hospital, or you did not have to be wired to several machines. Having a good congregation is a wonderful help in this difficult time – we were blessed with an amazing church family that provided us meals for six weeks after our second child was born. But no matter how wonderful other parishioners are, they are no match for homesickness combined with post-partum hormones. Even the best husband will not be able to give you enough hugs. God's provision through the means of grace is the only thing strong enough to deal with this trial.

Harder than giving birth from home or taking a child far from home is losing a child far from home. Through miscarriage, death, or rebellion and apostasy, losing a son or daughter when you are away from your parents, family, and old friends must be the most difficult aspect of homesickness, aside from losing your spouse. Burying a child is a terrible thing – burying a child beside strangers is a terribly lonely thing. Maggie Paton, too ill to attend her daughter's funeral, wrote to her family, 'I had to get the little Coffin into my bed! The Native Teacher laid it at my side, and fell down on his knees sobbing; while I got nearer to my God over my Child's lifeless body than ever I had done before in my whole life…He loved her, and loved her, infinitely better than I; and He could not be unkind.' In times like this, let the Atonement be your comfort: the God who allowed you to lose your child is the same God who gave His Child so that you could be redeemed and called by name; you are His. This dark valley can draw you close to your Savior.

8

Homesick and single

Being single and homesick can be rough. There is no one to share a new home with, no loved and loving people to bring with you, and all the work has to be done alone. Hudson Taylor, before he met Maria, suffered dreadfully from loneliness in the Chinese slums. One letter back home begged, 'Do please write. I have no letters, no *Gleaners* [a Christian periodical] – no papers – no companions… You would write [every post]…if you saw how disappointed I am when a mail comes and no letter.' He serves as an example to single men struggling with homesickness, with his three-pronged attack on this emotion: pray, work, pursue. Whether you have never been married, or are widowed or divorced, you can practice these three important things in conjunction with the suggestions above to fight homesickness:

Like every believer, and every homesick believer, pray that God would draw you closer to Him, make you useful for the kingdom, and provide everything you need to do this in your new location. Pray for Christian friends and mentors, and opportunities to serve with them. If you want a believing wife, then pray that the Lord would provide you with a godly wife who would be a helpmeet for you as you serve.

Work, for someone who is single, is different than it is for a married person. Paul points this out in his first letter to the Corinthians: 'The married man is anxious about worldly things, how to please his wife, and his interests are divided' while the 'unmarried man is anxious about the things of the Lord, how to please the Lord' (7:32-4). Live this out in dedicated service to the church. Utilize your singleness. After treating patients all day, Hudson Taylor would use the evenings to seek out other people and minister the gospel to them. Once your 'work' is done, go to the church, and pitch in there. This kind of self-sacrificing service will not only bless you, but it will also bless the church. Guard yourself against lonely, idle time.

Lastly, pursue. First, pursue strong friendships with godly men and families – people with whom you can fill the void of otherwise lonely time, transforming it into the safe haven of sweet Christian fellowship and accountability. Be active in cultivating solid friendships with other men. And if you are looking for a godly woman and meet one who seems as though she would be a good helpmeet for you in your work for the Lord, pray some more, get some counsel, and ask her out. Be aggressive: Hudson Taylor, decidedly not called to singleness long term, wrote repeatedly to a woman he loved and her father, proposing marriage several times. He later successfully pursued Maria in ways that could have been frightening to a girl who was not interested. If she is not interested, you will quickly find out – and that is a good thing. If she is interested, you find out quickly as well – also a good thing.

If you are a single woman in a new place, struggling with homesickness, you can also practice prayer and work. Pray that the Lord would sustain and bless you in this new place. Ask for His protection, guidance, and for provision of friends. If you want to be married, pursuing a man is not an option, but you can pray just as hard for a husband as a man can pray for a wife, and you can take up the Lord's promise that He will be a husband to the husbandless (Isa. 54:5). Work to befriend and be a blessing to families in your church. And you can pursue finding an older, godly woman to mentor you during your time in a new place, whether that is long or short. She will be an invaluable source of companionship, encouragement and, when you need it, rebuke. If you do get married, she will be an invaluable source of wisdom regarding husbands and children!

Whether you are a single man or a single woman, do not allow your loneliness to depress or consume you. Discontentment with your circumstances will not ameliorate the situation, but will only make it worse. Amy Carmichael, in reams of letters home, never once lamented her singleness. Instead, the letters are full of prayer requests for others, records of the Lord's blessings, and thanks for prayers and other help. She never married, but mothered hundreds of children in the faith. Her work for the Lord was incredibly fruitful. Hudson Taylor, who did eventually marry, flourished spiritually during his singleness in China. He was poor, very lonely, suffering from inadequate food, no sanitation, intense heat, and an unending stream of patients at his door. Through it all, he showed a devotion to God and a love for Christ that allowed him to serve effectively where the Lord had placed him. Being single and homesick is very hard, but it can also bear enormous spiritual fruit, in yourself and the community where God places you. 'Seek first the kingdom of God and his righteousness, and all these things will be added to you.' (Matt. 6:33).

9

Homesickness
in the pastorate

Moving to a new place to begin pastoring a congregation is an exciting thing. It is a fresh start to your
ministry, an opportunity to meet the spiritual needs
of the saints there, and a chance for you to learn
new lessons in the pastorate. But then, after a few
weeks or months, you realize that the congregation
is not what it seemed. Maybe there are factions,
maybe some people still want their old pastor, maybe there are cultural barriers to your work. If not,
ministry still presents the challenges of getting to
know a large number of people in a short amount
of time, attempting to understand and meet their
needs, and lead Christ's flock, even though you are
the new person. Finding a friend can be difficult –

you do not want to have 'favorites' in the church, but need some counsel and companionship to aid you in your work. Not to mention, you miss where you just left and are trying to help a wife and children adjust to the new setting.

Maybe you don't even understand why the Lord has led you to this place – you are obeying a calling without understanding it. Sometimes, everything is just getting comfortable in our lives, and for some reason the Lord calls us to move. He did this to the disciples at the end of Mark 1; people were just beginning to believe and flock to hear Jesus' teaching when He called the disciples to move on to the next town. There are probably lots of reasons the Lord has moved you, but you can be sure the biggest one is His glory and the spread of His kingdom. He has bigger goals than giving you a comfortable personal life. But this does not mean that He does not see and care about this trial that He has wisely given.

If you are a homesick pastor, then be encouraged! The Lord not only has abundant provisions of grace in store for you, but special promises as well. In response to Peter, who pointed out that he had left everything to follow Christ, our Lord said,

> Truly, I say to you, there is no one who has left house or brothers or sisters or mother or father or children or lands, for my sake and for the gospel,

> who will not receive a hundredfold now in this
> time, houses and brothers and sisters and mothers
> and children and lands, with persecutions, and in
> the age to come eternal life (Mark 10:29-30).

What a promise! And, like all of God's promises, it is 'yes and amen' in Christ (2 Cor. 1:20). Follow the Lord's lead, and He will bless. Preach the whole counsel of God, in season and out of season, and love the people. That is what the Lord calls you to do. Trust Him to provide the rest.

Also, be encouraged by the 'cloud of witnesses' that are already in heaven, having received the eternal life promised (Heb. 12:1). There is Noah, a 'herald of righteousness' (2 Pet. 2:5), called to build the ark while warning unrepentant sinners of judgment, then sent floating for months, priest to the only surviving people (Gen. 6-7). Think of Moses, leading the obstinate Israelites for decades, and doing it meekly, with no word of longing for the luxury he grew up in (Heb. 11:25). The disciples, especially Paul, travelled far and wide to preach the gospel to those who had never heard it. In church history there are countless pastors and missionaries who have, by faith, willingly left home and family to bring the good news of Jesus Christ to those who need to hear it. Hebrews speaks of those who have gone before:

> These all died in faith, not having received the
> things promised, but having seen them and
> greeted them from afar, and having acknowledged
> that they were strangers and exiles on the
> earth. For people who speak thus make it clear
> that they are seeking a homeland. If they had been
> thinking of that land from which they had gone
> out, they would have had opportunity to return.
> But as it is, they desire a better country, that is,
> a heavenly one. Therefore God is not ashamed to
> be called their God, for he has prepared for them
> a city (11:13-16).

Do not 'think of that land' where you used to be,
but put your hand to the plough where you are.
Allow this time of homesickness to drive you closer
to the Lord: to lean more heavily on Him, draw
more grace from Him, and serve more diligently
for Him. Also take the opportunity to minister to
your wife, grow closer to her, and encourage her in
her role in a new place. Show your kids some extra
love; teach them to love the new congregation. Use
your homesickness to pull you closer to your God
and the family he has given you.

Amy Carmichael lamented in her day,

> [W]e profess to be strangers and pilgrims, seeking
> after a country of our own, yet we settle down in
> the most un-stranger-like fashion, exactly as if we
> were quite at home and meant to stay as long as

we could. I don't wonder apostolic miracles have
died. Apostolic living certainly has.

Moving and homesickness can spur you on to
'apostolic living'. Instead of being a drag on your
ministry, moving and homesickness can actually
energize it when you gain a biblical perspective on
your situation and purpose. Just as the Levites had
no allotment of the Promised Land, but received the
Lord as their portion (Josh. 18:7), so you, moving
at the Lord's call, will receive Him as your reward.

If you are married to a man who has just moved
to minister in a new place, you can also claim Christ's
promise of other lands and family for your own. Your
ministry, ministering to and helping your husband, is
essential to the work, and the Lord will sustain and
even reward you for the work to which He has called
you. He will give you the grace you need. He knows
your frame, and remembers that you are dust.

But please take a warning with this encouragement. It can feel as though this new pastorate is your
husband's calling, and not yours. You feel called to
go back to where you were! But your calling is to
serve your husband, and do it, as all Christians are
called to serve, with joy (2 Cor. 13:11; Phil. 2:18,
3:1, 4:4; 1 Thess. 5:16).

When I was about ten years old, my father,
a pastor who had moved several times, invited
a pastor new to the area over for lunch. He brought

71

his wife. I do not remember what church they were from, what denomination they served, or what their names were, but I do remember that he tried to be cheerful and talkative. His wife said almost nothing, ate little, and had a heavy aura of melancholy about her. After they left, I asked Dad what was the matter with her. 'She wants to move back home,' he explained, and then added to my mother, 'She's going to kill his ministry here.' They were prophetic words; in less than a year, the church was looking for another pastor.

If you are tempted to behave like this, look to all the women, in Scripture and church history, who have followed their husbands near and far, facilitating rather than killing their ministries. Think of Sarah, leaving Ur (a city that even then had garbage collection) to wander in the desert. Scripture records her obedience to her husband (Gen. 12, 1 Pet. 3:6). Rebekah left her family forever to marry Isaac and raise children in the covenant line (Gen. 24:58). Leah and Rachel counted their father's house as nothing to go with Jacob (Gen. 31:14-16). David's wives led very itinerant lives while they waited for God to fulfill the promise of kingship to their husband (1 Sam. 27ff.). In the New Testament, Priscilla travelled with Aquila as he helped Paul on his missionary journeys (Acts 18:18). Many of the disciples had wives whom they took with them as they ministered in various places (1 Cor. 9:5). Add to that a few names from church history: Ann Judson, Maggie Paton, Susanna Spurgeon, and countless other women married to pastors and missionaries who facilitated their husbands' ministries, cheerfully bearing with moves, understanding that it was a small sacrifice they could make in order to spread the gospel. The Lord is able and willing to give you the same grace He gave them.

Considering the high calling you have before you as your husband ministers the gospel to perishing souls will bring clarity to the worst longings for home that you feel. Ann Judson, homesick to the core, recorded in a grueling mission post:

> Have been writing letter this week to my dear friends in America…The thought that I had parents, sisters and beloved friends, still in existence, and at such a distance, that it was impossible to obtain a look, or exchange a word, was truly painful. While they are in possession of all the comforts I once enjoyed, I am an exile from my country, my father's house, deprived of all society, and every friend, but one, and with scarcely the necessaries of life. These privations would not be endured with patience, in any other cause, but that which we are engaged.

Homesickness can be severe, with identifiable causes. But these causes are not greater than the cause for which you have left your former home and entered into Christ's service as a pastor's wife. The good news of the gospel is greater than any homesickness we can possibly feel.

My husband often reminds me, 'The cattle on a thousand hills are the Lord's. So are we'. Our Creator and Redeemer has the right to place us, move and remove us so that we can serve Him better. Separations from the people we love will force us closer to Him. Amy Carmichael wrote, on sailing away from a beloved friend to Japan, 'Jesus has two nail-pierced hands. He lays one upon each and parts us so – *He* does the parting.' The Hand that has parted you from beloved people and places for the sake of gospel ministry will sustain and guide you until that ministry is complete. Maggie Paton wrote to friends from the mission field, 'You would find it uphill work, indeed, to be sacrificing your whole life merely for the sake of those who cannot understand your motives, and who know not what it cost you to give up home and friends. But Jesus regards every sigh, and whatever is done for Him will meet with a sweet reward even in this life; for He who has promised can *never* disappoint!'

10

Staying in touch and going back to visit

If you have moved, you have heard the pleas: 'Stay in touch, okay?' 'Don't forget to write!' 'Let us know how you're doing!' And you have probably promised to do so. But staying in touch means different things to different people, and depending on how many friends and family you just left, it is likely impossible to keep up with everyone in the old location while connecting with people in the new place.

This might sound harshly impersonal, but after a move you will have to prioritize with whom you will communicate regularly. You cannot communicate one-on-one with everyone, so you have to choose wisely. Parents and siblings will likely top the list. After that, things might look different than you expected. Sometimes there will be someone whom you would like to stay in touch with, but they do not write back; someone else does instead. The most talkative person in your small group probably is not the one who will faithfully write you and pray for you. That is one of the ironies of moving; you find out who your real friends are. If someone does not write you back, do not waste your time banging on a closed door. Write the people who do write back. One friend wrote me 'old fashioned' snail mail letters the entire time I lived in Scotland; communicating this way was not only fun (it is always neat to get foreign stamps in the mailbox), but helped us to get to know each other in a way that we otherwise would not have.

If there is a group that you need to communicate with, then use a blog or newsletter-style updates to tell everyone what is going on in your life. Facebook and Twitter have made it possible to let a large number of people know how and what you are doing with a sentence or two a day. Just keep in mind that while people rarely share too little, it is easy to share too much over social media. Keep the personal stuff for the personal communication.

Remember that however many people you communicate with long distance, those relationships are no substitute for face-to-face interactions in your new community. This is especially true at church:

while you may keep in touch with people back home, you very much need to be in touch with the people of God where you are. Spreading yourself thinly by trying to communicate with everyone will lead to burnout. Instead, focus on those relationships that spiritually build up everyone involved.

Going back for a visit to where you used to live is great. It can also aggravate homesickness by reminding you exactly why you miss it all. Sometimes there are big disappointments. There are three main things to remember when you do head 'home' to help keep things in perspective and balanced.

First, remember that things will not be the same as when you lived there. Places change. Maybe there will be an ugly subdivision going up in the spot where a beautiful farm used to be. There might be an addition to your former church building that you need to navigate. Maybe the people who bought your old house need to cut the grass, wash the windows, and pick the toys off of the lawn. Your favorite restaurant could have new owners. That is how this world is: things change, and they do not always change for the better. Do not expect to return to exactly what you left.

People also change, which means that so do your relationships with them. Kids get big and forget who you are, teenagers go off to college, people get married, new families join the church, others move away, some people become ill, some die. But it is not just their situations that change – their personalities go through little changes. You might feel like a stranger when you come back to a family reunion, or a fellowship lunch at your old church. Remember that of all the people there, the one who has changed the most is likely you. Moving, especially when it is to a new culture or country, stretches you, teaches you, and refines you in a plethora of ways. The people you go back to visit have changed in different ways, and maybe smaller ways, so that you might no longer share as much in common as you once did. A man from Africa told my husband that the first time he went home after a year or two in America, he was deeply disappointed with the people there – he had subconsciously expected that they had all developed spiritually, doctrinally, and socially to the same extents and in the same directions that he had. Realizing that the disappointment was largely caused by false expectations on his part, subsequent visits have been far more enjoyable.

Your ideas about the Christian life may have changed in ways that people's back home have not. Maybe your old church seems legalistic and ingrown, or theologically loose and liberal. Perhaps your ideas about politics, child-rearing, or any number of issues have shifted, bringing potential tension when those topics come up during a visit.

Do not allow these secondary differences to destroy your relationships with other believers. Be humble. Do not expect to be able to bring everyone around to your point of view during a few days or weeks. God had to transplant you in order to teach you certain lessons – do not expect other people to learn them overnight, and remember that they will have learned other lessons that you have not.

Remember that if the people are believers, you will share even more in common spiritually, because sanctification always brings us closer to other Christians. When we go back to our 'old church', I am frequently amazed to see not only new faces but also the ways that people's spiritual development has jumped since I attended there. Though living far away means that I have a lot to catch up on in everyone's lives, it is a delight to discover that a sister in Christ has learned some of the same lessons that I have, or different ones that I still need to learn. So, expect to see changes in people, and look for new marks of grace for which to thank the Lord.

Second, do not try and visit everybody and do everything when you go back. It is not possible. Trying to do so will exhaust and frustrate you. Ann Judson, on a trip back to America after years of isolation on the other side of the world, attempted to visit with everyone whom she knew in New

England until she became seriously ill. To preserve her fragile health, her brother-in-law essentially kidnapped her, confining her to his home so she could recover.

My mother-in-law was the only one in her family to immigrate to Canada, so when she goes back to the Netherlands, there are a lot of people she could visit – childhood friends, cousins, people in the church, nieces and nephews, etc. But when she goes, she prioritizes whom she needs to see: 1) her mother, 2) her siblings, 3) any other family and friends who are willing to come and visit her if she has time. On occasion, she does visit old friends who are unable to come to her, but the focus is on her immediate family: the people she misses the most and who love her the most. Anyone else can do the work of arranging travel and visiting time to see her.

When my husband and I head back to visit a place where we used to live, we often make a list of things we would like to do when we are there, then pick one or two and focus on those. It might be going to the beach, taking the kids to our favorite ice cream store, or driving past our old home. They are small, entirely realistic goals because we know that time is limited and so are we. Picking and choosing usually means that you get to do one or two things well in between good visits with the people who are dearest to you.

The third thing to remember when you go back for a visit is to enjoy it. This might sound obvious, but if you are a mother you will know what I mean. You have to pack for everybody (don't forget shoes for church!), get the passports together, keep the kids happy during the car/train/plane trip, keep them neat enough to see their grandparents when they get there, try to keep a semi-normal schedule through the visiting, remember everybody's names at church (don't forget to congratulate the couple who just got engaged!), try to help your parents or friends where you can, apologize to the people who are putting pressure on you to visit them when you have no extra time at all, then pack everyone up and head home (don't forget the passports!). There is a lot of work involved in a trip. Sleep can be scarce in a strange bed. Not to mention, there are the expectations and emotional turmoil in visits like this – homesickness can rear its ugly head!

So relax. You are not going to be able to see everyone, do everything, and go everywhere, but the Lord has given you this opportunity to enjoy some of the people and places that you love. Enjoy it to His glory. Maggie Paton, after five years on a small island with mail delivered only once a year, travelled to Australia for a holiday with family from Scotland. 'I was, of course, wild with delight, and flew from room to room, all talking merrily.'

Knowing she had precious time with the people she loved, she determined to spend it in cheerful action, not crying to them about how lonely she was and how hard life had been.

Equally important, she remembered to remain cheerful when she had to leave, and return to the island: 'The Home-Coming was just delicious... there was on everything the flavor of originality which only the natives can bestow – for instance, sheets spread out for table cloths.' It is easy to see all the bad anew when you come home again; be thankful for the opportunity to visit, and put your mind to pray and work at fighting homesickness over again.

11

The good side of living far from 'home'

Homesickness is a side effect of moving far away from home, and it is a nasty one. But God gives us many enjoyable side effects, too. Though living far away from home is very hard, with lots of struggles and temptations, it certainly has its good side. Over the past year or so I have asked a lot of long-distance movers what they have discovered to be benefits of going off into the sunset and having to deal with all the work of moving. There are an awful lot! This chapter considers a few mental, emotional and physical 'perks' to living far from home, or moving frequently.

The very fact that you are homesick means that God blessed you where you were, which is why you are sad not to be there anymore. Even though these blessings have been taken away, you are still enjoying the benefits of past experiences and relationships. Moving can increase your appreciation for your old home. My sister, living in a university dorm in the eastern United States, wrote me, 'I am SO thankful for how Dad and Mum raised us! I had no idea it was abnormal!' Other people whom I know who have moved away from home become thankful for specific aspects of the old place – church, the market, a babysitter, playgrounds, modern plumbing, etc. Sometimes, you do not know how good you have it until the Lord removes you and gives you perspective. He can use a move to make you thankful to Him for blessings that you did not realize you had until you moved away.

I was once speaking to a South African about waiting with small children in line at the Department of Motor Vehicles in order to get an American driver's license. We had both done it several times. I commented that living in the same place for life must be so easy. 'Easy? Yes, easy,' the woman said. 'But really boring!' I had not considered this a positive thing before: when you move around, there is never a dull moment.

Moving often brings multiple needs. You will need money, energy, a place to live, a place to worship – any number of required things in order to make the move workable. Needs always allow the believer to see the Lord's amazing provision. We have been astounded at the multiple, often intricate needs that the Lord has met for us in each place. Sometimes, He provides before we even realize we have a need. For instance, when we moved to Scotland, people had kindly placed an elaborate stroller in the home where we stayed. When I saw it, I did not think I really needed one, but for months, that stroller was how I got groceries, walked the baby smoothly over stone streets, gardened with the baby watching from the stroller seat – how I did daily life. The Lord had given before I knew I needed. His amazing provision is an incredibly valuable lesson you learn from trekking around.

When you move to a new place, you get to see some amazing things. For one year, we lived in northern Virginia. In that time, we got to see nearly every major Civil War battlefield, the U.S. Naval Academy, Mount Vernon, the Baltimore Harbor, Chesapeake Bay, the Smithsonian museums and art galleries, the Cherry Blossom Festival, Luray Caverns, fall in the Blue Ridge Mountains, people sledding down the steps of the National Archives – things we would never have had the time or opportunity to enjoy even if we were there on holiday. There are so many incredible things to see and do in this world, and moving often allows you to enjoy more of them.

While you might get to see world heritage sights, oceans, capital cities, or mountains, sometimes the Lord places you in a home in the middle of nowhere, or in an ugly city. It teaches you to see the beauty in the small things. Maybe there is a tiny, flowering weed in the sidewalk that you realize is incredibly intricate. Or perhaps there is an upper-storey window through which you can see sunsets. When your life is in turmoil, pausing to focus on a small part of God's creation can help clear your head and remind you that the omnipresent God is good, no matter where you are.

You do not just get to see amazing things when you move around; you also get to meet wonderful people. When you move far away, the Lord introduces you to a new community of saints – brothers and sisters in Christ that you would never have met if you had stayed put. God often uses moving to expand your family. He adds the extended covenant family to the local church family. Instead of losing friends, the moving believer only gains more. God has blessed our family with people in many countries to whom we can go for advice, encouragement, and visits. We pray for them, and we know that they pray for us. That is a precious blessing that comes with moving.

One of the delights of being far from 'home' is to see believers with amazing stories of God's goodness to them, and the privilege of watching them live out the gospel in their particular cultural context. One of the beautiful things about Christianity is that it is not bound by time, place, or tradition, but rather that it transforms each of these things. When you move, you get to see how other believers live in their culture, raise their families, work and worship, conforming to Scriptural patterns while retaining unique cultural qualities. You get to see God's faithfulness in another part of the church. The gospel is not antithetical to racial and cultural diversity – quite the opposite! – and moving out of your home culture is a first-hand opportunity to watch and learn new things about the Christian life that you could only see by moving. We have learned different Christian customs as we have moved: ways that believers celebrate Christmas, or baptisms, or observe family worship. Seeing how another group of believers has biblically thought through an issue not only broadens your horizons – it makes you think through it more carefully as well. While we have not always agreed with a particular expression of the Christian life in some places, we have always been challenged to think through it ourselves, and been encouraged to see believers striving to know God's will for every aspect of their lives.

Going to a new place also opens up a new field of ministry for witnessing to unbelievers. A fresh start at relationship with people outside of the family of faith can be a chance to live more faithfully before them, speak of Christ more clearly to them, and learn to love the souls of men and women who have not heard or accepted the gospel. Moving is an enormous opportunity for Christian witness.

Moving also allows you to experience a culture, and all the foods, customs, holidays and lingo that go with it. Even within one country there can be many sub-cultures, each with something new to explore. We have been amazed at the variety even within the United States, from Rita's ice on the east coast to Chicago dogs in the midwest to fried corn-on-the-cob in the south, and that is only the food! Other dialects or languages can also be enjoyable: terms like 'chock-a-block', 'piggies', 'dummy', 'cheese head' (not to be confused with head cheese!), and *Je me souviens!* ('I'll remember!') have become part of our family vocabulary. We have also been able to experience totally random, a-cultural things, such as barbecued beaver at a fellowship lunch, or a waitress sitting down at our table and pouring out her heart to us. Living in another culture expands your culinary, literary, musical, architectural, and linguistic horizons.

Living far away also allows you to share your own culture with other believers. It is so fun to describe a Canadian winter to a Brazilian, or to feed an

American Christmas pudding, or to explain North American distances to someone in the Netherlands. And it can be a blessing to your new church and other believers to gain perspective on things like family worship, Christian education, or some other aspect of the Christian life that they had not considered. Moving not only brings you blessings – it also allows you to be a blessing to others!

Moving far away also takes you away from family and friends. Obviously – that is a huge source of homesickness, isn't it? But it is also a good thing. If you have a difficult family, this gives you time to get away and be by yourself or with your immediate family. God can use this experience to remove you from tensions and spare your children the influences of ungodly relatives. Moving may also remove you from being associated with secular lifestyles or even your own past. I know of a man who led a very wild life before his conversion. He drank, slept around, and had fits of violent anger. The whole town thought of these things when they heard his name. Moving away for work placed him in a new community that did not know this; his conversion coupled with his move gave him an entirely new reputation and start on life. His new community associates his name with hard work, Scripture memorization, and deep thankfulness to the Lord for his salvation. The move was an amazing blessing from his Savior's hand.

Even if you have a wonderful family and no ungodly past, moving can be a blessing. Living far away from them forces you to stop depending on them not only for help, but also for identity. The Christian community in Canada is relatively small and interconnected; I grew up with the refrain, 'Oh, you're _____'s daughter!' While in one way it is nice to have people make those connections, moving to Scotland meant that I could not depend on my family's reputation for people's opinion of me. If you move far away from your family, it is entirely up to you to create and maintain a godly reputation.

If you have ever given birth 'naturally', you will know how empowering it can be. Yes, it is agonizing, but once you are through it, you realize that you can do a lot more than you thought you could. Moving is the same. When you follow God's call to go somewhere, there is an awful lot of laboring involved. But God gives enough grace every time, and you realize that you can do anything that the Lord calls you to. This knowledge is energizing, even in the midst of homesickness. Getting out of your comfort zone can make you more fruitful in every sphere of life.

Moving to a new place can also mature your personality. A friend of mine was living in eastern Europe during a pregnancy. In the course of a routine trip to the doctor, she had to deal with an expensive taxi ride, a 40-minute wait in a hallway with smoking workers, additional delays inside the office, a second language, procedural confusion, nurses who were unconcerned with hygiene, a long bus ride home with a rude driver, heavy rain, and a worried husband. 'If it had been my first year there, I would have called my husband in tears at the first problem.' Instead, sanctified by months of living in a post-Communist setting, she took it all pretty much in her stride, and could even laugh about it when she told her husband how the afternoon went. I have found the same to be true. Moving around makes you grow up quickly.

It can also make you humble. Suddenly, you are like a child again, learning directions, names, new manners, maybe a language. You make mistakes, need a lot of advice and instruction from others, and are emotionally off balance. While these are hard things, they are good if they build your humility before God and other believers! Like a child who cannot reach the cupboard or keep the days of the week straight, you cannot do everything you want to, or remember all the experiences you are going through. Moving frequently has impressed upon me how limited I really am – physically, mentally, emotionally, spiritually – and how infinite God must be. Moving and homesickness put you in your proper, tiny place.

When I ask people about the perks of moving and living far away from home, one that they almost always respond with is a stronger marriage. Even if your marriage was good to begin with, a move can strengthen it. If your marriage was struggling, this is a good time to be gracious toward your spouse and try to develop a better relationship as you face so many changes together. In those first few days and weeks, you have no one but your spouse with whom to talk, work, eat, visit, and pray. Moving also teaches you things about your spouse that you would otherwise not have known. An entirely new situation can bring out new attitudes, opinions, abilities, habits, likes, and dislikes that you never knew existed. Whether they are positive or negative aspects of your spouse's personality, they will help you know each other better. Enjoyed or dealt with prayerfully, the experience of moving can be a tremendous boost to your relationship, as you grow closer together far away from everyone else. For weeks or months after a move, your spouse is the only one whom you really know and who really knows you; that creates deep oneness in a marriage.

While moving can strengthen a marriage, it can also create stronger bonds between parents and children. Mothers in particular, when they are married to busy husbands, can develop friendships with their children. A former missionary to southeast Asia spoke with me about how her oldest daughter – not yet in her teens – became a close friend as they both adjusted to a new culture, figured out daily routines, explored markets, and cared for the younger children together while the father was working. We moved and travelled a lot during my husband's doctoral studies, and I was often left with our child(ren) while he was in an archive. Exploring Cambridge, Princeton, Chicago, and other places with these little people has created memories and bonds that I would not otherwise have, and that I do not have with anyone else, not even my husband. Without becoming less of a parent to your children, moving can make you more of a friend. While moving makes your 'family' bigger as you meet and love other believers, it also makes the nuclear family much tighter, as rootlessness pulls you closer to each other.

Lastly, moving and being homesick can equip you to minister to others who are experiencing the same thing. In a world that is increasingly globalized and mobile, there are a lot of lonely people around, even in the church. If you have moved, and especially if you have been homesick, you understand what others are going through and can help them. One of the most encouraging things in a trial is to have someone who has endured the same trial come along beside you and empathize, comfort and cheer you. You can use your knowledge of the physical, emotional, and mental strain of moving to bless others who are dealing with homesickness.

God is so good to give us a list of perks this long! Each person and family will have their own list of blessings that come from moving; writing them down and sharing them with family and friends can be a wonderful antidote to homesickness. These sorts of blessings are benefits which would be difficult or impossible to have while living in the same place. It is so true that in the Christian life, gall comes by the teaspoonful, honey by the gallon.

12

Homesickness:
a wonderful reminder

While there are a lot of positive aspects to moving around, the biggest ones are spiritual. The best thing about homesickness is that it points us to heaven and the Savior who waits there for us. When we are done this earthly pilgrimage, we have a heavenly home waiting for us. On the way, the Lord uses homesickness to sanctify us and make us fruitful as we walk towards the eternal city.

Homesickness reminds us to make the most of the time we have. You used to live in one place, and now you live in another. Someday, you will leave where you are now, and go to another new place, whether on this earth, or in eternity. Use homesickness as a reminder to make the most of the time you have where you are.

Paul encouraged the Ephesians, 'Look carefully then how you walk, not as unwise but as wise, making the best use of the time, because the days are evil' (5:15-16). Enjoy God's blessings, welcome the stranger, serve in the church, use your gifts, share the gospel, and do it with zeal, because you do not have forever. Even a long life is 'a few handbreadths;' our lives are 'nothing' before the Lord (Ps. 39:4-5). Leaving a place with regrets for things undone and unsaid will be hard not only because of the pangs it causes you, but also because you know you have squandered a precious gift from the Lord: time. One thing my mother taught me in her moves was to serve to the maximum possible, to the point where you can look back and say, 'I did the most I could with the time and energy God gave me – I could not have done any more'. Let homesickness be the catalyst for God to teach you to number your days and so gain a heart of wisdom (Ps. 90:12).

Each move, I have gotten rid of a lot of stuff while packing. Some of it is garbage, some of it gets passed along to other people, and the rest gets put into boxes. You empty a house, you leave a house. Some are pretty, some are comfortable, some we only love for the associations we have made with them. Regardless, moving and homesickness remind us that this earth is temporary. When we die, we cannot take anything with us, just as when we move we cannot take everything with us.

When a friend of mine was going from Eastern Europe to California, this truth came home to her in the airport as she and her husband struggled to carry everything they owned; they left a pile of stuff on the airport floor, freeing themselves from unnecessary luggage, and blessing an airport worker with some clothes. Let homesickness teach you to hold the things of this earth with a loose hand, blessing others with what you have, and willing to let the rest go. As my grandmother says, 'It's all going to burn'. Do not store up treasures here, 'where moth and rust destroy and where thieves break in and steal, but lay up for yourselves treasures in heaven' (Matt. 6:19-20). For 'we brought nothing into the world, and we cannot take anything out of the world' (1 Tim. 6:7).

Homesickness is a reminder that this earth, with all its stuff, is not our home. Heaven is. Joel Beeke says, 'You are merely a renter here; a mansion awaits you in glory.' Homesickness is preparation for that Place and the wonderful things God has in store for His children there.

Homesickness is also a reminder to prepare very specifically for dying. To a modern westerner, that sounds morbid. But it is biblical. Ecclesiastes 7:1 even tells us that the day of our death will be better, if we are prepared in Christ, than the day of our birth. Every time we relocate, leaving a home and things and people we love, it is like training for death, when we will leave this earth forever, and go to a home that we will never leave. In past centuries, missionaries would often ship their belongings in a coffin, expecting to use it themselves when their work for the Lord was done. It was a reminder that death was certain, and that they had work to do before it came. When a move comes close, just as when death comes close, we put our paperwork in order, clean out the house, and say goodbye to the people we love. Use every move to prepare yourself for the last goodbye. We need to long for heaven and prepare for heaven while we serve on earth. If we do not remember that we are ambassadors from heaven to earth, we will be ineffective servants in the kingdom. Comfortable life in a wealthy country can often obscure the reality that we are dying creatures living in a fallen world. Homesickness brings that spiritual truth into clearer focus.

Moving far away from family and friends can also teach us to rely solely on Christ for everything we need. Ann Judson, wandering from America to India and through southeast Asia, lamented in her diary:

> It seems as if there was no resting place for me on this earth. O when will my wanderings terminate? When shall I find some little spot, that I can call my home, in this world? Yet I rejoice in all thy dealings, O my heavenly Father; for thou dost support me under every trial, and enable me to lean more heavily on thee.

God can take us away from people we love in order to bring us closer to Him. Every time we move, leaving people we love and depend on, it causes us to lean more heavily on Christ: the only Person we ultimately need and whose love is the only love that will go with us even to the uttermost. Even a wonderful husband cannot meet every need, especially when you are homesick. But your Maker is your Husband (Isa. 54:5), and He will provide everything you need for life and eternity. As David Brainerd wrote, 'Lord, I'm a stranger here alone;/ Earth no true comforts can afford./ Yes, absent from my dearest One,/ My soul delights to cry, my Lord!' Being away from other people we love can make us love the God-Man more.

This world is under a curse. That is why being away hurts. We have inherited Adam's original sin, which is why we tend to respond sinfully when we feel homesick. But God has reached down into this cursed world in the person and work of Christ not only to forgive that sin and sanctify us, but also to bring us to heaven. John Piper reminds us that because of Christ's intercession on our behalf, 'We are no longer strangers and sojourners. We have come home to God'.

That knowledge can cheer us while we are here; it can comfort us when we feel homesick. There is Someone who left His home so that we could spend eternity in His. Every pang of homesickness should point us to heaven, which we will never leave, and which we will enjoy with everyone else for whom

Jesus died. More than that, we will spend all of our time in our eternal home praising the Savior who brought us home. There is an old hymn that goes,

> I need thee, precious Jesus for I am very poor;
> A pilgrim and a stranger, I have no earthly store.
> I need the light of Jesus to lead me on the way,
> To guide my wand'ring footsteps, to be my strength and stay.
> I need thee, precious Jesus, and hope to see thee soon.
> Surrounded by the rainbow and seated on thy throne.
> There, with thy blood-bought children, my joy shall ever be
> To sing my Jesus' praises and gaze, dear Lord, on thee.

When we do long for home, we can remember that it is coming. In fact, remembering that this earth is simply the believer's road to heaven can make this earth a place of springs, and enable us to go from strength to strength until we arrive in the eternal Zion (Ps. 84:5-7). For the Christian, the best is always yet to come, and meditating on eternity will help put this in perspective. Time on this earth, no matter how many places we spend it, is short; eternity is vast. Mary Winslow reminds us that 'We are here for a little while, soon to appear at Christ's bar. Live for Jesus – live for Eternity'.

13

Helping someone who is homesick

If you are someone who has said goodbye to a family member or friend and you realize that they are homesick, you may be at a loss as to how to help them, especially if you have never moved yourself. Here are some suggestions that may help you minister to a sad child, sibling, parent, or friend.

Most importantly, pray for them and tell them that you are doing so. Wherever they are, whatever their situation is, what they need most is the Lord's sustaining grace as they cope with all the challenges in a new location. Pray that they would grow closer to the Lord and find comfort in Him. Ask God to provide a good church, and to enable them to bear a lot of fruit where they are. Pray that they would be able to see and enjoy all the blessings of a new place. Pray that they would have the physical strength to go through all the packing, travel, unpacking, and sleeplessness that so often comes with a move. If there is a new language involved, pray that God would give them quickness of mind to learn it. If the homesick person is married, ask the Lord to use the move to bless their marriage. If they have kids, pray that they would have tender wisdom in helping the children adjust quickly. Pray that the Lord would give them good friends in the new location. And remember to thank the Lord for His providential dealings; His ways are higher than our ways, and whatever He ordains is not only right but also good.

You can also help someone who is homesick in person. When a friend tells you that they have decided to move, do not express shock and horror that they would think of moving away. It is always a difficult decision, and they have spent much time to arrive at it. If you think it is a foolish or even sinful choice, there are loving, gracious ways that you can communicate your concerns. Comments like, 'Oh, that's going to be so hard – it's so far away from your mother!' are profoundly unhelpful. Instead, assurances of prayer, offers of help, and other encouragements are useful.

Try not to be horrified if the place where they are moving is distant, difficult, or strange. At one point, my husband applied and interviewed for a job in Macau. The gambling capital of China was not exactly top of my 'where-I-want-to-raise-children' list. When I told my mother that my husband was being interviewed for the position, she could have moaned with me, been sad about the grandchildren possibly moving to the other side of the planet, and commented on how hard it would be. Instead, she very selflessly and helpfully said, 'What an amazing opportunity! The kids will learn Chinese, you'll be able to eat amazing food, *and* be part of what the Lord is doing in China!' That helped me see the opportunities ahead, instead of the obstacles.

When you have moved far away from people whom you love, they are always in your thoughts, but you often wonder if you are in theirs. Getting an e-mail, message, or phone call can be a great boost. A letter in the mail is even better than an e-mail, because it says that you took the time to sit down, write, address, stamp and mail a note. All of these things take planning and some effort, which communicate that you were thinking of the person far away.

When you write or call, have positive things to say; encouragements in the Lord, funny anecdotes from your daily life, helpful questions about what they are experiencing and enjoying. Especially encourage them to build and maintain new relationships with other believers, and to settle into a good congregation.

Help them think through their situation and become a catalyst, even from far away, to help them settle in and enjoy where the Lord has placed them.

Sending a package is also a thoughtful encouragement. One of my sisters, living a few hundred miles away from home at college, received an unexpected package in the mail from friends one day. It was some candy, a note, and a flash drive full of pictures – simple, but it made her week. Those sorts of gestures are an amazing blessing.

Try to keep a homesick person updated on what is going on in your life and the church. One of the frustrating things about living far away from people whom you know and love is that you get left out of things that you should know. Occasionally we have gone back for visits and discovered that someone is expecting, has been diagnosed with cancer, moved, or joined the church; it can be embarrassing to deal with this information on the fly in a fellowship hall. While you cannot involve someone who has moved away with your daily life, do try and notify them when something significant happens.

If you can go and visit, that is an amazing way to encourage someone fighting homesickness. One of the things that creates a feeling of being disconnected after a move is the knowledge that nobody who really knows and loves you understands where you are living and what it is like. Having family and friends visit is a special blessing. Everywhere we have lived, people from our former congregation have taken the time and effort to come and see where we live and talk with us. In one state, we had half the congregation come and see our family!

It is not just the visit itself that is helpful, but the knowledge that people can see your situation, give you some perspective, and maybe a little help. Visits from others have also forced us to find the fun things to do in every place; we want our guests to be able to see something unique during the visit, so planning for their arrival has made us become more familiar with the new location. It has also made some wonderful memories, from climbing in ruined castles with my siblings to finding a fast food place in a ghetto with friends. If you are close to the person who has moved away, a visit is the ultimate way to demonstrate your care for them.

When the person or family comes back for a visit, one simple way you can help them is to not put pressure on them to visit you specifically. They probably already feel overwhelmed by too much to do in too little time; pushing them into a visit with you (even if they do like you) is going to be unhelpful, and perhaps damage your relationship. When we were planning one trip back to a former location, a friend asked if we could come for dinner. I told her that I was not sure what our schedule would look like yet, aside from that it would be packed. Very thoughtfully, she wrote back, 'No pressure. If it doesn't work out, we will see you at church. Just know that you are loved.' That sort of thoughtfulness is so kind, and a lovely gesture to someone who is homesick.

If you meet someone who has recently moved to your area or church, the best way to help them is to connect with them. Invite them over for a meal and do family worship with them. Ask them to go on a day trip with you so you can really get to know them. Try to find out their birthday so you can drop off a card, some flowers, or a gift when it rolls around. Involve them in your life and become involved in theirs. What a homesick person most wants is to know and be known; to have people who understand who they are and still love them. Be willing to be their friend.

Connect with a new person spiritually; pray for and with them, invite them to a Bible study or your small group. Ask them about their conversion, where they have come from ecclesiastically, and what God has taught them through this move. A spiritual connection is one that is not only helpful in battling homesickness, but also one that matures people in the faith.

Give a newcomer your phone number and e-mail address, and let them know you are ready to answer any questions that they have. Aside from emotional support, someone who has just moved needs a lot of help finding a doctor, figuring out a transportation system, locating an office supply store, and other orientation. Be there to answer questions willingly and cheerfully, even if it is not convenient for you.

Involve a homesick person in serving others in the church, community, or both. In one congregation where we landed, the pastor's wife approached me a month or two after we had arrived, asking if I would host the annual Christmas tea for women in the church. This was not only a great way to give me a project that would benefit the church: it also allowed me to get to know a lot of women, and let them into my home to know me. Do not be afraid to give a new person a job to do; it enables them to be a blessing and become part of a community.

Reaching out to newly arrived people who are not believers is an especially strong way of showing Christ's love to a stranger. Christian love is a powerful way to not only help someone battle homesickness, but also to address their spiritual condition. Get to know them, pray for them, invite them to church – do whatever you can to show Christ to them. Warm Christian hospitality is an especially attractive presentation of gospel love.

Even if the new person does not seem interested in your attempts to welcome them, they probably are, and it will be a blessing to them. Whenever we move, I tend to switch into 'survival mode' – unpacking, doing paperwork, analyzing, evaluating, and trying to remember new names. I come across as very disinterested in other people, even though I enjoy getting to know other believers. So do not be put off by someone who seems shy or stand-offish or shell-shocked. At the seminary where my husband teaches, it is often the most serious, diligent students who need the most interaction and cheerful encouragement.

Someone who is homesick needs people to reach out to them. So if you know someone who just moved away, or someone who just moved in, reach out to them, and pray that God will use you as an instrument of blessing in their lives.

References

Alcorn, Randy in Shel Arensen, *Come Away: How To Have a Personal Prayer Retreat*. Grand Rapids, MI: Kregel Publications, 2003.

Beeke, Joel R. *Practical Lessons from Puritan Theology Today*. Grand Rapids, MI: unpublished manuscript, 2011.

Brainerd, David in Vance Christie, *A Flame for God*. Fearn, Ross-shire, U.K.: Christian Focus Publications, 2009.

Cromarty, Jim. *It Is Not Death to Die: A New Biography of Hudson Taylor*. Fearn, Ross-shire, U.K.: Christian Focus Publications, 2001.

Duncan, John. *'Just a Talker': Sayings of John 'Rabbi' Duncan*. Edinburgh, U.K.: Banner of Truth Trust, 1997.

Elliot, Elisabeth. *A Chance to Die: The Life and Legacy of Amy Carmichael*. Grand Rapids, MI: Revell Books, 2005.

James, John Angell. *A Help to Domestic Happiness*. Morgan, PA: Soli Deo Gloria Publications, 1995.

James, Sharon. *My Heart in His Hands: Ann Judson of Burma*. Faverdale North, Durham, U.K.: Evangelical Press, 2003.

Mackay, George Leslie. *From Far Formosa: The Island, Its People and Missions*. New York: Flemming H. Revel Company, 1895.

Paton, Maggie. *Letters and Sketches from the New Hebrides*. Grand Rapids, MI: Reformation Heritage Books with Sprinkle Publications, 2003.

Piper, John. 'Strategic Hospitality' (http://www.desiringgod.org/resource-library/sermons/strategic-hospitality, accessed February 23, 2012).

Ray, Charles. *Mrs. C. H. Spurgeon*. Pasadena, TX: Pilgrim Publications, 2003.

Thurber, Christopher A. and Edward Walton. 'Preventing and Treating Homesickness' in *Journal of the American Pediatric Society*. Vol. 119 No. 1 (January 1, 2007), 192-201.

Christian Focus Publications

publishes books for all ages

Our mission statement –

STAYING FAITHFUL

In dependence upon God we seek to impact the world through literature faithful to His infallible Word, the Bible. Our aim is to ensure that the Lord Jesus Christ is presented as the only hope to obtain forgiveness of sin, live a useful life and look forward to heaven with Him.

REACHING OUT

Christ's last command requires us to reach out to our world with His gospel. We seek to help fulfil that by publishing books that point people towards Jesus and help them develop a Christ-like maturity. We aim to equip all levels of readers for life, work, ministry and mission.

Books in our adult range are published in three imprints:

Christian Focus contains popular works including biographies, commentaries, basic doctrine and Christian living. Our children's books are also published in this imprint.

Mentor focuses on books written at a level suitable for Bible College and seminary students, pastors, and other serious readers. The imprint includes commentaries, doctrinal studies, examination of current issues and church history.

Christian Heritage contains classic writings from the past.

Christian Focus Publications Ltd,
Geanies House, Fearn, Ross-shire,
IV20 1TW, Scotland, United Kingdom.
www.christianfocus.com